PRAYERS
for Uncertain Times

Peace + joy!

PRAYERS
for Uncertain Times

Robert J. Wicks

Paulist Press
New York / Mahwah, NJ

Cover photograph by Doug Ferraro
Cover design by Joe Gallagher
Book design by Lynn Else

Library of Congress Cataloging-in-Publication Data
Names: Wicks, Robert J., author.
Title: Prayers for uncertain times / Robert J. Wicks.
Description: New York / Mahwah, NJ : Paulist Press, 2021. | Summary: "Prayers for Uncertain Times are selected and new prayers, reflections, and dialogues all under one cover in a brief work that is easy to carry along during the day. With the conviction that a creative use of imagery allows us to surface a sense of God and self in a vivid and personally compelling way, Wicks also offers readers a straightforward process to write from their spiritual experience and thereby embrace holiness in prayer and action"— Provided by publisher.
Identifiers: LCCN 2020048518 (print) | LCCN 2020048519 (ebook) | ISBN 9780809155507 (paperback) | ISBN 9781587689482 (ebook)
Subjects: LCSH: Prayers. Classification: LCC BV245 .W46 2021 (print) | LCC BV245 (ebook) | DDC 242/.8—dc23
LC record available at https://lccn.loc.gov/2020048518
LC ebook record available at https://lccn.loc.gov/2020048519

ISBN 978-0-8091-5550-7 (paperback)
ISBN 978-1-58768-948-2 (e-book)

Published by Paulist Press
997 Macarthur Boulevard
Mahwah, New Jersey 07430
www.paulistpress.com

Printed and bound in the
United States of America

ADVANCE REVIEWS FOR
PRAYERS FOR UNCERTAIN TIMES

Deep-hearted prayers authored by a person with a loving spirit, certain to draw you into a peaceful, hope-filled abiding. These refreshing prayers will stir deeply within your being and linger long after you have held them close to you.

Joyce Rupp
Author, *Anchors for the Soul*

This collection of prayers and reflections reads like poetry and song, inviting the reader to recall that God is always near, especially in the most uncertain of times. With the skill of an artist and the wisdom of a sage, Dr. Wicks brings to life the spiritual themes near and dear to his pastoral heart: compassion, self-care, resilience, and true prayer. This is a collection worth reading, reflecting over, and praying with time and time again.

Daniel P. Horan, OFM
Duns Scotus Chair of Spirituality
Catholic Theological Union
Author, *God Is Not Fair and Other Reasons for Gratitude*

Selah! This book of *Prayers for Uncertain Times* enables, I, the pilgrim, to break from the stressors in my life especially during the current pandemic journey that has visited our world. *Selah*, a Hebrew word used seventy-one times in the Psalms, invites me to pause, be still, and listen. The reflections from within the pages of this book transcend the messiness of our pandemic world and quietly travel with me toward harmony and peace within. No doubt that after reading and praying this book of prayers I feel an even greater closeness with our Lord in these uncertain times.

Most Rev. F. Richard Van Handel Spencer
Auxiliary Bishop
The Archdiocese for the Military Services, USA

Dr. Wicks' deeply felt free-verse prayer poems invite us to sit quietly with our gentle God who persists in asking us at every sunup and sundown and each moment in-between: "What do you need?" and "How can I help?" His cosmic view of our personal and communal place in ordinary time that is no longer ordinary and may never be again reassures and refreshes the whole person.

Rose Pacatte, FSP
Author, *Corita Kent*
Founding Director
Pauline Center for Media Studies

For Eugene Hasson,
a dear friend, a fine priest, and a good soul

CONTENTS

INTRODUCTION

Why This Collection, *Now*?

For my whole life, my work has revolved around encouraging—especially in professional helpers and healers—an appreciation of the following:

- *Compassion* as a "circle of grace" in which you sense God's call, as well as share Divine mercy when reaching out to others;
- *Self-care*, because you can't share what you don't have;
- *Resilience* so you can deepen, rather than simply bounce back, from stress;
- Gaining, maintaining, and regaining *a healthy perspective*, because if your eye is good, your whole body will be good (see Matt 6:22); and
- *True prayer*, because real spirituality dawns when God becomes as real as the problems and joys we face each day.

I have traveled across the country and lectured around the world as part of these efforts, in such cities as Beirut, Phnom Penh, Port au Prince, Budapest, Sydney, Auckland, Toronto, Guatemala City,

Belfast, Manila, and Hanoi. During these presentations on the above five areas of personal growth, I have noticed a common response: With persons living through especially difficult situations, the approach that seemed to truly resonate with many was the integration of psychology and spirituality. They wanted God to become more real in the challenging and, paradoxically, rewarding days in which they were living.

I noticed as well that when I wrote posts, columns, and articles on themes to encourage the simple care of a hopeful heart, the ones that would secure the most animated and grateful responses were ones in which I offered a prayer from my previous works on spirituality or had created new ones for the moment in which all of us were struggling.

With these reactions in mind, I decided to select prayers, reflections, and spiritual dialogues that I wrote and included in past works, as well as to compose new ones, to offer hope, encouragement, and direction in the uncertain times we are going through now. The goal I had was to finally put selected and new prayers all *under one cover* in a very brief work, which would be easy to carry along during the day.

Prayers for Uncertain Times is the result of this effort to provide support to make life richer, compassion greater, and perspective clearer. In the case of post-traumatic growth, some people don't merely bounce back from the adversity they face. They become even deeper because of the very challenges they are facing—paradoxically, in ways that would not have been possible *had the trauma and serious stress not happened in the first place.*

The same has always also been spiritually possible when facing a true sense of darkness. In such instances, when we don't play down the tough turns in life that we face and yet are simultaneously open to where they may take us spiritually, we open ourselves up to new possibilities in the interior life that were previously considered impossible. When this happens, true prayer welcomes this spiritual depth in quiet, little ways, as well as in a more dramatic sense. In walking with God when in doubt, while feeling lost, or experiencing uncertainty, the darkness will be no less, but the new light can surprisingly change things in amazing ways going forward. Such a result, marked by a *different* spirit of gratitude, understanding, simplicity, and humility, can all be in the offing—in *the* Spirit.

When we pray and ask God to find us again in surprising ways amidst the darkness, the portal to a transformed Divine relationship is seen in new ways under different circumstances. Accordingly, how we live our life going forward is made new. *All things are made new*. With true prayer, nothing less than this should be sought and much more than this is possible. That is the belief at the heart of the prayers, reflections, and spiritual dialogues that follow.

PRAYERS,
REFLECTIONS,
DIALOGUES

Find Me Again, Lord

There are so many times You have found me
that I can't even recall all of them anymore.
One moment, I'd find myself feeling all alone
and, the next, You would be at my side.

But now, I need You to find me again, Lord.

Let me know
You are there in the splash of a goose landing in water,
the noise of a city at night,
or in the quiet of a still forest.

I need You to find me again, Lord.

Help me know You are thinking of me
in the way someone offers a smile,
in the care expressed in a note received,
or simply in a cup of coffee, slowly enjoyed.

I need You to find me again, Lord.

Possibly the tears quietly sitting on my cheek
will remind You once again of me.
Maybe the giggles of a child or broad grin of an old friend
will have me recall Your presence once more.

But whatever it might be,
I need You to find me again, Lord.
To whisper my name in some way
so I can feel Your intimate presence.

Yes, I need You to find me again, Lord...*soon*.

Creating a Place God Can Call Home

When Jesus was born, he had a certain destiny
to make this world
a place God can call home.

As part of this journey
he called people to become
partners with him in its creation.

This meant helping all of us realize
that this world we live in is actually
the beachhead of the "kin-dom" of God.

Today, as we continue to experience this call
we may experience not only friendship and love
but also greed and hate.

We may encounter not only hope and open arms
but also, those who would trade the joy of community
for the "security" of ME-first.

But still our smile never need completely disappear
nor the search to seek Jesus' goal
ever totally cease.

Because the desire for inner peace remains too great
and the love for community too powerful,
to stop seeking to create *a place God can call home.*

Come Sit by Me

When I am tired God says,
"Come sit by me."

I speak about the little
things that have happened to me
during the day
and I am heard.

I share my fears,
angers, doubts,
and sorrows,
and I am held.

I smile with what energy
I have left
and am gently teased.

Then when all the conversation
is over and the day has been
opened up
and emptied out,
I am ready for rest.

Nothing is solved.
Nothing is under control.
But nothing pressing remains.

And as I go to sleep a fleeting thought
breaks the smooth surface
of my peace:

What would I do each night
if God didn't say,
"Come sit by me?"

The Circle

O God, there is so much pain
in the world.
Where do I begin to help?

"Start in your circle."

But when I help
my family and friends
often they really don't appreciate me.

"But I do."

And when I reach out
to my coworkers
some suspect my motives.

"I know what is in your heart."

Still, I think I should do more
to help those I don't know
who are suffering in the world.

"Then widen your circle."

But by myself I can't
do much to lighten
their great darkness.

"Yes, I know. That is why I am with you."

If only I could believe
You are with me.
If only I could *really* see You.

"Open your heart
in prayer
and you will see."

Please tell me what will I see?

"That as you walk
through the day
I am the center of your circle."

Let Me Remember

O gentle and caring Spirit of Life…

When I feel frustrated by someone's ingratitude and
   seemingly impossible expectations,
let me remember his neediness or fear of saying "Thanks."

When I face a person's rage,
let me remember the pain she has long endured at the hands
   of so many others so I can give her the space to share her
   anger freely and without fear.

When someone sees the world (and me) in extreme negative
   or positive ways,
let me remember that I am neither horrible…nor, for that
   matter, am I omnipotent.

When people are very troubled, and I begin to feel
   overwhelmed by it too,
let me remember that "simply listening" is in itself truly a
   quiet, great grace.

And when I see a person making the same mistakes over and
   over again,
let me remember, that sometimes I'm not such a winner
   myself!

Yes, as I sit with others who are sad, in pain, under stress, depressed, anxious, and afraid,

let me remember the Spirit of gentle faithfulness in this world, so I can be present to others the same way Your Spirit always is to me.

The Garden

I want to walk in the Garden
and have You as a companion,
as my grandmother and grandfather did before me.

So You can softly encourage
and help me avoid the stones
that trip me when I'm alone.

I need to hear the birds sing
together with Your voice
in the shade of the old trees

and see Your smile
as the sun touches the flowers
and makes their faces laugh.

Yes, I can't walk alone in the garden.
I need You at my side
just as my grandmother and grandfather did before me.

Snow Falling on Snow

In a cozy little corner
I sit and pray,
wrapped in a warm sweater
with a candle lit
before a mysterious icon.

Outside, the snow is swirling,
the wind is whooshing
and the tree branches scratching
against the house,
wanting to come in.

Then, in the spaces in between,
when the wind is forgotten
and all is quiet…
I open my heart
to listen.

And as I hear the peaceful sound
of snow falling on snow,
my soul slowly softens…
and my worries retreat
to the edges of my room.

Finally, I realize with joy
that no matter how uncertain life may become,
I will always be safe and warm
when I am with *You.*

Kneeling in Silence

Most of the time I pray and sing
while sitting or standing straight.
But now
the only way to release my soul
is to gently kneel and wait.

Ordinarily a few spoken words
would open up my heart.
But now
to hear Your gentle voice
deep silence needs a place.

My soul is now too lonely
to hear just spoken words.
And sitting or standing
before You
no longer bears my faith.

So, I quietly kneel
in reverence
until Your Silence comes
to touch the sadness in my soul
and to heal me...once again.

Softening the Soul

Lighting a candle
in a dark room
is a small gentle act of peace.

When the match touches the wick
time slows down
and the race to the future ceases.

Worries are consumed,
anxiety burns out,
and I sigh...*deeply*.

Watching the flickering light
is a graceful prayer
which eases my stress and lessens my strain.

Finally, when the flame goes out
I turn quietly back
to the events of the day

and find everything changed because of the time
I sat softening my soul
...by candlelight *with You*.

A Small Dark Chapel

As I enter a small dark chapel
I feel I'm returning home
silently welcomed by Someone
who expected me all along.

Taking a seat in a back row
I settle for a time
to enjoy the glow of candles
and rest here for a while.

The incense of an earlier hour
still lingers in a haze
with a scent so softly present
there's mystery in the air.

Then in my mind's eye
I clearly begin to see
the joys and tears of others
who prayed before me here.

They sat on wooden benches
and shared their doubt and pain
thankful they could come in need
to find peace once again.

And as I leave I'm grateful
that I've come here as well
to find silence and some healing
in this small dark chapel…God calls home.

Evening Prayer

Now, as I watch the fading soft colors of dusk,
I pause, breathe deeply, and remember You.
My heart is tired, yet I am filled with hope.
My body aches, but my spirit is at home.

As I stretch and lie down for the evening,
let my worrying cease,
my tired muscles relax,
my plans wait for morning…
My heart be at peace.

Yes, let me sleep in Your arms
until a fresh, clear morning awakens me
so I can greet You with love…once again.

Nurturing a Hopeful Heart

Read a bit

Listen to a favorite song

Call a friend

Remember a kindness

Help the poor

Keep perspective

Smile broadly

Laugh loudly

Close doors gently

Do what you can

Live gratefully

Relax for a moment

Breathe deeply

Tease yourself often

Take a quiet walk…

Tell God a funny story

My Hands Were Full All Along

I met an older woman who had little
and asked how she was.
The answer she gave me was so surprising, it woke me up.

"I am overwhelmed with so much goodness," she said,
"not because I prayed for more but because
instead I prayed for gratefulness."

After this encounter, I suddenly felt the cool breeze
in a way I hadn't before.
You see it was delicious and suddenly I was refreshed.

And now I am like a child again
and remember to look up more often
to see how the clouds entertain the sky with joy.

Then, when I am in a city
I can feel the great energy
alive in the streets.

In the country I cherish the peace
and how the birds laugh at the squirrels
and nature entertains us all.

The gift she gave was space to really listen
not simply hear people out
while waiting for my chance to speak.

Then, out of the blue I experienced a true surprise,
someone *really* listened to my story, too!
And, I also felt heard by someone who knew.

Next, I took time with my coffee,
time with my music, as well.
Even time reading a bit each night, something I rarely do.

I am fortunate that I have prayed for more gratefulness.
That I even knew to pray for this grace.
Who could have known what joy it would bring
    to my inner space!

In walking through the door of gratitude
I noticed something that makes me smile.
I don't own more than before but been given
    so much I missed.

Dear Spirit of love, help me to pray each night
and every morning without fail
so true gratitude will always prevail.

A World of Reverence

As I walk in this world far from home
You remind me that
reverence leads to awe.

I sit in a small Bangkok café
and watch a young man stop and pause
to gently touch an orchid growing along the road.

At a Mass in India a priest takes off his shoes
before the consecration as a sign of true respect
for the miracle that is next.

On a cool afternoon in Hanoi
I watch an older woman bow before placing
a cold glass of water before a statue that is there.

In an Orthodox church in Hungary the priest pauses
and incenses the altar for all of us present
as a way of letting us know we too are honoring God.

Thank You for waking me up to reverence
in these ways I might not have noticed
at home.

Please accept my gratitude
for rituals of awe.
May many others see them as well.

May all of us also worship You
in how we live with awe
so all we experience we can thankfully place...at Your door.

The Surprising Night

Dear Creator God, when life becomes dark
I am tempted to try harder
but You call me to be present to a spirit of patience.

When I become anxious,
my natural desire is to run away
but You gently and firmly ask me to stay.

When friends and family fail me
or I let them down, I want to cry
but You ask me to forgive and move on.

And, when I am tempted to hold on
only to what I can see, You ask me to have faith
and look again so I can let go and be free.

Your darkness is not an end but a beginning.
Not an abandonment or the end of life
but quite simply, the beginning of a new one for me to embrace.

One in which I can express gratitude for the Light
and a willingness to learn in the night,
so I can believe and travel where I haven't gone before—

A place in the surprising darkness
where You will meet me anew
and I will find new humility, wisdom…and *You.*

The "Little Things"

O God, when I feel overwhelmed,
help me to appreciate the "little things"
as You did when You faced adversity.

I know You are calling me forward
and at my side because
You urge me on to:

> smile at others
> call a friend
> laugh with a child
> stop for a chat
> take a short break
> recall good times
> be grateful for the morning
> listen to lonely neighbors
> buy someone flowers
> share some candy
> donate to a good cause.

Thank you for urging me on
in these simple ways,
dear God.

I already feel the little things
melting the discouragement
deep within my heart.

The Communion of Saints…
Here and Now

I am surrounded
by love, wisdom, fun, and comfort.
Let me see them more clearly, O God.

You send me *prophets…*
let me allow them
the freedom to awaken me.

You surround me with *cheerleaders…*
let me embrace
their sympathy and love more tightly.

Harassers who show up when I need them…
let me laugh more freely as they tease me
so I don't take myself so seriously.

You lead me to *inspirational* friends as well
who call me to be all that I can be,
without embarrassing me for being where I am.

Let me hear all their voices,
follow their lead, and
count them among my communion of saints.

The "Conversion" of Paul...and Me

When Paul was knocked down
and he was made blind

we call it
the "conversion of Paul."

But he didn't
leave the scene

singing I am blind
and now I can see.

Instead, he was
moaning...

I thought
I could see,

I thought I knew God
...but now am blind!

Lord, so many
of us think we can see

and condemn others
who don't agree.

Help me to keep
my own eyes open

so You can
reach out and

teach me
again.

Because in meeting
You

without having a dynamic
faith

and not a fixed religious crutch
that doesn't grow with me

I will forget
our relationship

must *constantly* be renewed
to remain alive and true.

Help me not to settle
for comfort
when Your joy awaits me.

It may seem safer to
remain blind

and believe
I have all the answers.

Yet, to humbly accept
that I often don't know

is the real gift of Light
in the midst of darkness…

in life
my life.

If only
I can remember that…

that is all I ask,
that is all I pray for,

so I can have the inner space
to welcome You

in new amazing ways
especially when I need You the most.

The Final Calling

When I was young You asked me
to step forward
and not put my "light" under a bushel basket

so, I looked for my charism,
saw it as a name You gave me
and then sought to feed it so the gift would grow.

When I was in my forties
You called me again to see my light was
    too bright
so I looked for another gift to cut the glare.

And now, I hear Your final calling
to take the quiet gift of my forties
and make it a central focus going forward.

So, as I was passionate when young
and gently passionate as a young adult,
now, I feel called to more fully embrace gentleness
    as my own.

When I do this, I find the grace
of a calling like no other
it frees me to know it is not my reflection
    but Yours that I seek.

I know this is right because I feel freedom to simply be
without wondering what others are thinking
or believing, about me.

Maybe I can help others find their charism too
and know when to prune it until
You call them as you did me to embrace
    their final calling as well.

A Personal Beatitude

In turbulent times, let me go up the mountain with You.
Teach me the Beatitudes anew so I can sit with Your disciples
and learn.

I know that You blessed the poor,
they who mourn, the meek,
those who hunger for righteousness, and the merciful.

I know You embraced the pure of heart, the peacemakers,
the persecuted, the strangers,
and those who were maligned for your sake.

I do know this, O God.
In a way I already feel rewarded by Your love now
as in heaven.

Yes, I do know this all.
But what I don't know is my *exact* call to action
during these uncertain times.

I have climbed the mountain in prayer.
There is a sense of community as I sit with Your disciples.
But which beatitude is assigned to me now?

I seek to walk with the poor,
the pure of heart inspire me to act,
but which *specific* calling is mine now?

I ask not out of guilt
nor to be a success
or even to be seen as "helpful."

No, I want to know exactly what You want
because if I can find it more clearly,
I know that is the place where I can give You my best.

Homesick

When I make rounds in the hospital
and see invalids vainly trying to
turn to relieve their pain…

    I am homesick for simple kindness, O God.

As I see the disproportionate
number of people of color in prison
feeling no sense of power…

    I am also homesick for equality.

While I walk past the working poor
trying to make ends meet,
have a little joy, and keep their families safe…

    I am homesick for justice, as well.

Then, when I hear religious persons like myself
judge others harshly based on principles
without the presence of love as a guiding Light…

    I am truly homesick for mercy, too!

May prayer bring me to the home of compassion
so I can live with You in this messy world
with a sense of kindness, equality, mercy, justice…

    and, yes, love, O God.

A Surprising Companion Sent by God

O God, an author I know
once said,

that he knew everyone
must die

but thought that somehow,
in some way,

he would
be an exception!

When I am sick
and feel weak,

when I receive
an unexpected diagnosis

or a friend dies
and the world doesn't stop,

hopefully, I will see death
sitting by my side because

I now know he is not there
to make me sad.

She is not there
to bring me down.

But the image of death is present
to wake me up

to who and what is fresh
now before me

in ways I couldn't appreciate
before.

When I know death is
the constant companion You have sent me

I won't be surprised
when it all ends.

Instead, I will
be always awakened

each day
when dawn comes

and I hear you say,
"I give you…

one more day,
one more opportunity

to enjoy life
by being gentle

and good to others
who have also

been given this gift
of one more day."

Thank You, again, O God,
for this chance and

for sending me
such a memorable companion

so I may not be forgetful
or only see daily tasks as "a life"

but instead am alive
to…*each* day,

every day,
in a gracious way.

Amen.

Spiritual Sadness

Sometimes You come very quietly,
so silently that if I am not silent enough
I don't hear Your voice.

The same is true
when I am sad during the day
and it only seems gray in passing.

The feeling isn't dramatic.
It is not depression for sure
and it certainly isn't dark night of the soul.

Still, it is a time when you are visiting.
If I pay attention, I know You will
have a message there for me.

And so, O God, help me see my sadness
as a portal to something more
so when I feel hurt or low

You will teach me something *more*.
More about what I am holding onto
that is less than You.

More that is greater than my reputation
or the ideal image I wish for
and spend so much energy chasing.

Yes, in the sadness of the day
let me see that more than everything else
this lesson teaches me more about Your unfailing love.

Amen.

Help Me with My Memories

I need to visit my memories
again
but, this time, please come with me, O God.

I must go back because
if I don't go there the memories will stay
quietly within and lead me on

without me knowing where or when.
You see, the memories forgotten
are the only ones with power

for they have quietly
driven me to do and say things
without me knowing their way.

But this time, please come with me,
where I can feel Your love
so there is no need for me to run away

and miss the lesson there.
For even when I have hurt someone
all is not lost in the fallen past.

Instead, there is a chance for
forgiveness
and a place to humbly smile.

Because honesty will open up space
for me to now forgive others, too,
as You have done for me.

The memories of the past
are never all pleasant
and there are many faults to note

but there is also love
hiding behind them
that want a chance to be known.

So, this time please come with me,
and help me see what I have done,
and missed, in the near and distant past.

Not so I can simply feel guilty
at where I have failed others,
myself, and You.

But also to find where I have loved
or been present in the moments
that have brought people joy.

Yes, I am ready to return
to the past without a blind eye
so I can see everything.

In this way my memories
will be blessed whether pleasant or not
because You have come with me, O God…

and that is all that counts.

Amen.

An Unexpected Invitation!

Normally I only
attend Mass
on Sundays.

I enjoy the chance
to meet *You*
in the Eucharist, the Word, and all present.

But, recently
I have found myself
participating at daily Mass.

What a joy to feel the quiet
and receive a quick reflection
on the message Scripture holds.

Starting the day
this way is different, though,
not lively like Sunday.

Instead, the daily encounter
turns my morning
into a mini retreat.

And, now when
I ask myself,
How did this all start?

I lean back
and need to laugh
at myself

because I realize
it was obviously an unrequested
invitation from You.

Thank you!
What a nice surprise to be given.
What a simple great grace to receive...*and embrace.*

Which Way, Lord?

During these times of hate
I find myself lost and confused.
Please help me…which way, Lord?

As I walk through
Your day, I try not to
avoid the messiness,

the place
where the Holy Spirit lives
and thrives for me and others.

But how can I
find my way
in that confusion

with so many choices,
needs,
and demands?

There is no
clear path or goal
that will let you preach to me loudly.

> *Just begin on the road to humility*
> *and turn next on vulnerability*
> *when you see the sign.*

What will I find there, Lord,
that will then
lead me on?

> *You will find*
> *the wide boulevard*
> *you truly need in your life.*
>
> *It is the Sermon on the Mount*
> *that I gave as a guide*
> *a long time ago.*
>
> *But know that people ignore it,*
> *change, or take part of it*
> *and seek to leave the rest.*
>
> *They turn at one*
> *side street and shout*
> *I have found the truth.*
>
> *But that's not*
> *what I asked of them*
> *to live in a good way.*
>
> *You must hear*
> *the whole Sermon*
> *and seek to follow it all.*
>
> *Start with the beauty*
> *of the right to birth.*
> *It's a beautiful beginning.*
>
> *Then continue*
> *to listen to the*
> *rest of My story*

and don't take a "religious"
way out before
I bring up the poor,

the suffering, persecuted
the pure of heart,
and the rest of my friends.

I never said following it
would be something
easy or direct.

Yet, being simplistic
is not what I need.
Instead, I desire an embrace

of all the Beatitudes
and not to make
one "god"

to let you escape the call to decide
what and who is right in the moment

that your conscience can own
even though you are troubled
with what you have chosen alone.

No, the Sermon
I gave gives direction
that's broad

in a world
that is messy
yet filled with reward.

You must face
the broad demands
of the Sermon now

and not run away
to hide behind one truth
letting the rest fall away.

Yes, I will walk with you
in the messiness
and you will feel it, too.

in the Holy Spirit's gift
of knowing you're involved
by being hated at times

by those
who don't want the pain
of embracing it all

and fail
to hear the whole Sermon again
and know it's My call.

No, turning your back on the poor
and letting children and the stranger suffer
no matter what good you claim will not be your answer.

Instead, enter the messiness of life
with the Spirit at your side
and you will find your way and more than that…the Way.

Welcoming a Scriptural Spring

At Your urging I read the book
on Your relationship
with Your people
in Sacred Scripture.

And as I began searching it,
all is quiet until
I start
asking questions of it:

What does this mean?
What is the Bible claiming?
But instead of answers,
the Scriptures start questioning *me*:

Who are you reading these Words
and how is your life a gift to others
now that you have begun reading them
with your identity on the line?

All of a sudden
my life leaves its winter
and a new spring
arrives.

My eyes are opened
and each day breaks
my heart anew with its unique
surprising beauty.

No longer were the Words
from a distant past
but instead cut the emotional chains
of a limiting secular present.

How nice to have
spring, again.
How moving to see You
this way.

I'm smiling at every part of my day.
Now my spiritual and scriptural spring will be forever
…even in the falls, winters, and summers
of my life.

Thank you for this…thank you, Adonai,
for the nudge to really read Scripture
but this time with both my mind and heart
so in uncertain times, I now have a place to renew.

Opening the Gifts of Spirituality

Creator God,
help me open
the gifts of spirituality.

When I do
I am not
of this world

but
truly live in it as You would have me.
So, I seek:

> Smaller steps instead of grander gestures
>   and greater speed
> Better health, not more "medicines"
> Time to listen and less to speak
> To be awake in the moment, not have a longer life
>   to merely exist
> Unlearning so I have space within for new wisdom
> Greater patience, not a quick, sharp tongue
> Values to live by rather than morals
>   to preach loudly to others
> Appreciation of family and friends *now* who I
>   recognize won't be there forever
> To be kind—especially to those who see me as a model
>   for their own behavior

To avoid splitting people into good and bad based
    solely on whether they meet my needs as I want
    or demand them to
To eat and drink slowly and enjoy fully all that I have,
    not simply what we rarely enjoy
To honor what is physically in front of—not only
    virtually available to—me
To take time for silence and solitude
    and being wrapped in gratitude before God
    so the quality of my life and love can be purer
Being less judgmental and more compassionate
The courage to let go when a person needs to move on
    with others
To appreciate more the value of waiting and patience
    in place of rushing, becoming frustrated
    and unfilled
To deepen my relationships rather than counting my
    "likes" or "followers" on the web
Praying more in spirit than only in words
Simplicity instead of complexity
Contact rather than being enveloped
    in a field of thoughts or ear pods
Membership in a small group, not a large chat room
Satisfaction with what is in front of me,
    not wasting time envying what is on a menu
    of something beyond me
Meditation rather than undisciplined activism

Yes, if only You would,
help me open
the gifts of a richer spiritual life

so *all* of my life
has peace and joy at its core
and the beauty of love never experienced before…*ever before.*

Time Off

Thank you, Redeemer God,
for the new space.

Prayer has released me
to take off time to live.

The few quiet moments
in the morning

have radically
changed each day.

The spiritual "air" surrounding me
and whom I meet

has become different.
so I can now hear the music

that makes me smile
because I'm looking with clear eyes

instead of how
the world wanted me to see.

Yes, I am taking
time away
from a life of unnecessary worry
and preoccupation.

And the result
is really astounding

because the
still photograph

I used to call a day
has been put

in a box
where it belongs.

Instead, now, with
morning prayer

I really have
the time off I need

to enjoy
a real experience

that is my life
now.

Thank You, once again
for the new space

and the different life
that comes through prayer.

My Childhood Died Today

Today, I visited my old neighborhood
and walked the streets of my youth.
I looked at the house I was raised in
and the yard I played in as a child.

I then passed in front of the houses
of dear friends from the past,
I had lost touch with a long time ago,
and felt the joy that we had together.

So, later I went on the web
and searched to bring them to life again.
I didn't expect to see much there
since they had led quiet but good lives.

But instead I found their death notices
and sat quietly alone.
I tried to tell others about how deeply I felt
yet failed to achieve understanding.

You see my childhood died today
and only You know I've lost it forever.
Still, the peace I have now is seeing
You know my feelings and embrace me, dear God.

You, not just I, know the days are fleeting
while "the now" is a forever moment
that can't disappear
when I am with You.

Yes, my childhood died today and I learned
    that You understand
how I felt and am happy now to know more deeply
that You are with me in the beginnings, the endings

...and forever.

Why Compassion Is "Simple"

I asked a friend who was compassionate
how he could be so kind.
He answered,
"How much effort does it take to sit down next to people
and help them cry?"

To another person whose life was crumbling,
I noticed a real change for the better
and asked,
"How did you change so completely?
Before you were lost and now seem found."

She replied,
"God led me to meet a gentle and good person
and I watched how she sat with me.
Then I began practicing
sitting with myself in the same way."

To yet another, I asked how she could journey
with the poor who had been traumatized.
She responded, "I know I must enter
their darkness with them
but I lean back enough because I know
    something special about love."

"What is that?" I asked and she replied,
"The opposite of detachment is not compassion as people think.
It is contamination of our spirit which brings us both down.
You see one of the greatest gifts I can share with others
is a sense of my own peace but I can't share what I don't have."

I was stunned and asked all three:
How can I be compassionate like them?
You see, it still wasn't clear to me.
Then they all answered in unison,
"Three things!"

"Know that:
Compassion is simple.
Success is not important.
Instead, faithfulness is.
But, of most importance, know

compassion reminds us to do what we can
but also to always remember
we are not alone
others will help
and God will certainly take care of the residue

in God's time
in the Redeemer's way
and
with Divine love."

And so,
compassion
is
as simple
as that.

Prayer to Little Children Who Have Passed

This prayer was inspired by a presentation I delivered many years ago on resilience and self-care for the Association of Pediatric Hematology/Oncology Nurses at Memorial Sloan-Kettering Cancer Center in New York City. It is dedicated to nurses caring for children with cancer and their families.

Dear Children, as I sit with your nurses and doctors
in the pediatric unit of the hospital
for cancer patients where you stayed,
their pain seeps through and falls on me.

My eyes are now opened more
as I see their suffering
at losing your life
after hearing your laughter.

Your parents have wet eyes
and sob and scream as well
while remembering your trusting look
that all would be well…that all would be well.

Now, I also think of you little ones
who have died.
Will you hear
all of our fervent prayers now?

Will you help us know you are well so we can let go?
Will you allow us to move on
with you in our hearts
so we can share your bright smile with others in need?

Dear Children, your parents will not forget you *ever*.
Dear Children, the physicians, nurses,
   and people you touched,
including me, will also remember you…
always.

Please smile down on us now
as you did so often in life
and continue to remember our tears and loss
as we recall your laughter and fun.

Yes, please don't forget us
and embrace the prayers we send to you.
We need you to know we will remember you
in blessed different ways forever…*please remember us, too*!

The Waves Wouldn't Leave Me Alone

This morning I came to the shore
simply to sit and ignore…but the waves
    wouldn't leave me alone.
Time and again, they would come
and rinse my precious worries away.

I really just came here to look over the horizon
to quietly be and not to experience a miracle
but Your waves just wouldn't leave me alone
and Your breeze decided to also come
    to blow my troubles away.

I didn't ask for relief, but the water was cool to my feet
and the air was so delicious that I had to remember
    Your love again.
Coming to sit by the ocean, I had no expectations, no goals,
    for me.
Yet, You came with plans to rinse me clean and make me
    smile again.

I had *no expectations* for my trip to the shore
so you saw this was the chance to teach me:
Being open in life with no demands
was just the right setting for prayer.

Thank You for showing me miracles can happen wherever I am
and that all you ask is for me
to be attentive to the many ways
You are already present to me.

Lessons from Two Famous Unexpected Storms

I sat in the boat's bow with an expert sailor by my side.
It was quiet so I smiled as the sail bellowed and pulled us on.
All was peaceful and joyful for me to experience
the deep silence and almost solitude.

Then life's wind and an unexpected storm suddenly came up
and with it I felt turmoil somehow
in a way I hadn't experienced before
so my face shared worry as well as some of my fears.

In response, the expert seaman smiled at me
as the water rose to the edge of the side of the boat.
He then showed me how to capture the wind and trim the sail
reminding me of another storm a long time ago.

I then asked myself at that moment why I was worrying
and had as little faith in You as they did long ago.
This didn't calm my seas.
That would be humanly impossible.

No longer was I on my first sail though.
No longer was I in turmoil
or feeling You needed to be shaken
and awakened as in my heart.

Because my faith was deeper now—
not that I had total
security, comfort,
understanding, or answers.

No, I had none of those completely,
but I did now have the kind of faith
that had room for doubt, uncertainty, losses, and fears.
Now I had made room for the belief that You would always
    be there.

Community of Unrecognized Gifts

O God, help me to clean my lens
so I can not only see my faults
but also the gifts I have been given by You
that I have ignored or not fully recognized yet.

I have spent so much time
working on developing the main gifts
You have given me to share
that I haven't been thankful enough
     for the others that are there.

Help me also recognize these other gifts
will actually prune the ones I know well
so they will blossom even more fully,
at the right time, in the best way, as well.

And, that when I explore and offer
all my gifts they will help others, too,
to have the courage to explore all of theirs
so *our* community of unrecognized talents
     will flourish *together*.

This will hopefully be for Your glory,
in gratitude to You,
to help us express more completely,
the hopeful community You want us to be.

Unmasking the Dark Demon

Today, people are fearful
so they focus on an enemy without.
I try to reason with them
but their hurt wins out.

They feel it's best to divide
and get people on their side
to hear a reaffirming echo
of their pride.

They seek to find those against them
so they needn't look within.
I now realize much more clearly
it's the same with me as well.

Even though I don't want to be angry
I am as guilty as others who shout.
But my anger is much more quiet
so it keeps itself silently inside rather than out.

Now I know anger is neither a demon
nor is it especially good.
It is simply a true challenge and sign
of possible evil whether thrown out
    or wrapped tightly within.

Awaken me to its presence even in my dreams
as well as when speaking out loud
so I can be free of hurtful anger
before it grows into horrible hate.

Waiting for the Past to Change

So much time is wasted waiting for the past to change.
I stand on the doorstep of possibility
    and see others do the same.
I review my memories not in an effort to learn
but to avoid passing through a new spiritual portal
while waiting for the past to change.

I could be embracing gratitude
but fear my hurts will then be forgotten.
I could be smiling at what others have given me
rather than demanding only more
while waiting for the past to change.

Yet, there is a chance now, O God,
for me to embrace forgiveness
and move on in life.
Still, it is scary for me to let go
while waiting for the past to change.

Please give me the humility to see past gifts,
and what others have given me with good will
so I have the courage to love and be grateful,
rather than waiting for the past to change.

I no longer want to remain alone,
quietly filled with entitlement on the doorstep of my life.
Yes, please help me to walk through the portal
    of new faith and hope,
instead of wasting my life by simply waiting
    for the past to change.

Wow!

Wait until you hear what happened to me, Lord.

Last night the rain put me to sleep.
The morning sun made me squint with glee.
I then had a hot delicious cup of coffee
and sat with a big smile on my face.

The rest of the day opened with a nice walk
and I waved at a neighbor leaving home for the store.
Plus, a quiet drive after
just made the walk's pleasure linger more.

I opened the door to my office,
closed it back up for a bit
so I could remember Your kindness
to me as I took a moment to quietly sit.

Following this, the day held more new chances
for me to be of help.
Each person I encountered needed something.
So, following You, I gave of myself.

Once again, when I felt lost
I took a quick additional walk
only to find You and know
that You were walking as well.

Are You sure all of these gifts
that Your day can bring
are really mine to enjoy
and fully there for me?

I almost can't believe
all of this can be true.
What a gift to be gifted,
alive and free.

Would You help me to remember
these presents again when life is tough
so I know that I am never alone, forgotten
and lost?

I want to always be grateful
and be able to pray once more,
"Wait until you hear what happened to me, Lord,"
so I can feel really free.

So, each day that I am alive
I won't forget or miss enjoying
Your goodness, surprise, or gifts
but instead simply as a child of God exclaim…

Wow, how wonderful
Your graces and gifts are…
Are You sure they're
all for me?!

The Second Miracle

Walking along the ocean for my whole life it seems
I was suddenly greeted by a surprise
causing me to stare.

This time it was a first,
a sand dollar was lying there.
Never had I seen one whole on the shore to hold in my hand.

I immediately thought
it would make a deeply felt gift
for my daughter to remember me when I am away.

So, I brought my prize home
to let her know
I remembered her and provide her a way to remember me.

Yet, I noticed the sand dollar wasn't perfect.
It had some dark scars
scattered here and there.

And so,
I decided to wash it clean
and I did it with care.

Still,
I broke it and stopped to stare
at the pieces left in my hand.

I realized it was delicate,
now nothing was left but sand
and I expected to be a bit sad

But instead
to my surprise
I actually cried my gift was gone now.

I had seen a miracle
and failed to honor this gift
as it was.

I saw an imperfection
and needed to make it right and clean
but failed to see clearly what it might mean.

All of life has smudges.
They are part of true existence
along with the hurts and stumbles we have along the way.

I am glad I didn't miss
the second miracle
I was given now

to see the connection
between imperfection
and the wonders of a life.

That God loves us
with our blemishes
as well as our faults.

This gift was a reminder for me
we can follow suit and love others
who are, like us, imperfect, just the same.

In this way we can share
the wonders of the world
instead of crying over broken sand.

And so, the real miracle for me was the second one
because this one didn't break
because it was accepted and held gently in my hand.

Thank you, again,
for letting me see this
because there is so much more I now won't miss.

My eyes will not solely focus on the blemish
and there's so much more because of You
that I won't miss now…Hurray!

Lord, Am I Willing?

Lord, am I willing to not rush to judgment about people whom I find tough to be with?

Lord, am I willing to set my expectations for others aside so I have room for hope that You will do something with them in ways I might not see?

Lord, am I willing to let people not like or understand me as I would desire but instead have the kind of patience with them that You continue to have with me?

Lord, am I willing to realize that compassion includes self-compassion?

Lord, am I willing to gently attend to my own inner life through spending some quiet time with You each day so I can share Your presence with others by attentively listening to them rather than to my own needs at the time?

Lord, am I willing to be accepting of myself when I fail or become too concerned at times with my own image?

Lord, am I willing to really believe in the power of prayer, so I am not sidetracked by my own fears, anxieties, desires for a quick solution, wish for appreciation, or aversion to negativity, trauma, and loss?

Lord, am I truly willing?

Help me to experience You in the midst of times when I
   encounter sickness, poverty, stress, anxiety, depression,
   misery, and sadness so I am not tempted to run away,
   harshly judge, or become depressed and helpless myself.

That is what I ask.*

* Source: Wicks, Robert J. *Conversation with a Guardian Angel: A Novel* (Cincinnati, OH:
Franciscan Media: 2015). Used with permission.

Prayer

Things are so much clearer
since I met You.

Honesty seems sensible.
Friendship comes easier.

My senses are sharper.
Hope is understandable.

Understanding is desirable.
Joy is spontaneous.

Sadness is a wise teacher.
Even death makes me curious.

You know what?
I think we should get together more often!

Meals of Life

The waiter brought a beautiful meal
looking so delicious it made me smile
but I didn't eat it and let it get cold
while I looked off in the distance
thinking of something else.

Seeing this, the waiter looked
perplexed but said nothing ill to me
just simply looked sadly
and took it away almost untouched
and certainly unenjoyed.

The next day he brought
an even more tasty dinner
and I rejoiced when I saw it
because I had missed the first one
and here was yet another chance.

However, like the first,
and the second,
the third,
as well as much of my life,
I did the same.

Until I realized the meal
I had been given by God to enjoy
would soon be gone
without me having
really tasted any of it at all.

Then I went back to my life
and the waiter smiled at my return,
gave me another meal,
and saw me enjoy it
to the full!

Smiling and laughing
as she took away each plate,
each one as empty as the one before
until she took away the final plate
and the angels began to sing.

A Question…
What Are Tears For?

They…

Bring to the surface
feelings that are hidden below
so they don't remain invisible
and quietly harm where we go.

Help us see what we really value,
hold onto,
live for,
and call precious.

Wash away our illusions,
sense of permanence,
attachments and comfortable
imaginary independence.

Clean and clear us within
so we have room to see
friendship in a new light
and God in a deeper way.

That's some of what
the wisdom of sadness
and the purpose of tears are for.
What else?

EPILOGUE

Creating *Your Own* Prayers and Reflections

For those who have read my books or heard me speak, reading most of the prayers, reflections, and spiritual dialogues in this book would not surprise you. They contain the themes that are dear to my heart. So, why include them here again in this format?

There is a twofold reason for this. First, I have tried to keep them very brief. People today are so often tired and overwhelmed with so much to do. They need something brief to read as they start or end their day. In this way, the themes can be remembered and seed the day or be carried into their dreams at its end.

The other reason is that prayers, reflections, and spiritual dialogues create imagery in ways that simple prose often cannot. In reflecting this way, we are admitting that the spiritual life is more than mere thinking *about* God or reciting a set of fixed prayers created by someone else.

A creative use of imagery allows us to surface a sense of God and self in a vivid and personally compelling way. The poet and Anglican divine Thomas Trahern put it beautifully when he noted back in the 1600s that

> you never enjoy the world aright till the sea itself flows in your veins, till you are clothed with the heavens and crowned with the stars, and perceive yourself to be the sole

heir of the whole world; and more so, because men are in it who are everyone sole heirs as well as you…till your spirit fills the whole world, and the stars are your jewels, till you are familiar with the way of God in all ages as well as with your walk…until you delight in God for being good to all, you never enjoy the world.

There is a place for clarity created by confronting distortions in our thinking and perception. Likewise, there is also a need to see the "gods" we worship as a result of facing our unexamined false beliefs. These may include perfectionism or a desire to be viewed by others in what we deem a favorable way.

With imagery elicited in the process of preparing personal and communal prayers and reflections we seed our own inner life. In the spirit of Jesus' parable of the wheat and the chaff, Thich Nhat Hanh rightly points out: "You don't need to directly encounter the seeds of your suffering; you can plant new seeds that have a healing nature. In other words, you can seed the unconscious."

Moreover, as seminal thinker and psychologist Arnold Lazarus accurately states in his book *In the Mind's Eye*,

the use of imagery can often bypass verbal roadblocks and get to the root of the matter. Many people tend to over-intellectualize and they confuse everybody and themselves with verbiage.…*Find* the images and you will understand the behavior. Furthermore, find the images and, if you so desire, you will probably be able to *change* the feelings and behavior.

In line with this, as I said in a previous book of my own, *Touching the Holy*, what most of us fail to realize is that we are using imagery all the time without even being aware of it.... This does not mean that imagery can replace knowledge, but what it can do is put that knowledge to work more effectively, because if the script we are operating on has a good image of self as its basis, then the negative will be edited out and the positive emphasized.

This process of creating prayers and reflections opens us up to see what within and without is preventing us from embracing *imago Dei*, our being made in the image and likeness of God, and being more truly compassionate toward others as a result. So, when we create prayers to share with God, written for no other reason than being in covenant with the Divine, we can open up and be free in ways not previously possible.

The objection often given to writing prayers and reflections, or creating dialogues between yourself and God, is that it is too hard. Another claim may be that I am not creative or bright enough. However, if the song "The Drummer Boy" means anything—he can only play *his* drum and song—then like him, the gifts we each have are sufficient for the task. As a matter of fact, quite simply, for each of us they are the *only* ones that are.

A THREE-STEP PROCESS FOR WRITING

Offer yourself and your gifts as you seek to join your spirit with *the* Spirit in this process of reflection:

1. Find a quiet space or one where no one will bother you during your writing, while also relaxing yourself.

2. As you relax, reflect on what during the day has meant something to you. You are setting the stage to speak with God.

3. Then simply write to God about your reflection on the day, as you would write to someone else who is close to you.

YOUR FOCUS FOR WRITING

- Don't worry about grammar, correctness, or anything else other than to share your feelings, thoughts, perceptions, joys, fears, hopes, anxieties, and surprises.
- Experience the power of uncovering your feelings and cognitions (ways of thinking, perceiving, and understanding) without censoring them or feeling too foolish to write about them; this can help you discover what is motivating you in life.
- When you uncover and share this with God, at the very least, it is out on the table. You are, in contemplative Thomas Merton's words, uncovering the false self and seeking out the true self before God.

Such a process of reflecting and writing can turn your activities in life into a "pilgrimage" like the one taken by the saints and characters of God before you. Why not join in this journey? Especially in these uncertain times, it will be a way to touch the holy in yourself and the world around you, no matter what difficulties are occurring or uncertainties there are. This is just what is needed now in this world—an embrace of holiness in prayer and action.

As Kenneth Leech noted in his book *Invitation to Holiness*,

> To recognize holiness is to recognize the activity of God in people. More than that, holiness manifests the character, the nature of God....Holiness never points to itself but always beyond itself to God. The saint is essentially someone who communicates and radiates the character of God, his love, his joy, his peace....And the world needs saints, Simone Weil wrote, just as a plague-stricken city needs doctors.

To this, I would only add: *Amen.*

ABOUT THE AUTHOR

For more than thirty-five years, Dr. Robert Wicks has been called upon to speak calm into chaos by individuals and groups experiencing great stress, anxiety, and confusion. Dr. Wicks received his doctorate in psychology (PsyD) from Hahnemann Medical College and Hospital, is professor emeritus at Loyola University Maryland, and has taught in universities and professional schools of psychology, medicine, nursing, theology, education, business, and social work. In 2003, he was commencement speaker for Wright State School of Medicine in Dayton, Ohio, and in 2005, he was visiting scholar and commencement speaker at Stritch School of Medicine in Chicago. He was also commencement speaker at and the recipient of honorary doctorates from Georgian Court University (Lakewood, New Jersey), Caldwell University (formerly College; Caldwell, New Jersey), and Marywood University (Scranton, Pennsylvania).

Over the past several years, he has spoken on his major areas of expertise—resilience, self-care, and the prevention of *secondary* stress (the pressures encountered in reaching out to others)—on Capitol Hill to members of Congress and their chiefs of staff, at Johns Hopkins School of Medicine, the U.S. Air Force Academy, the Mayo Clinic, the North American Aerospace Defense Command, the Defense Intelligence Agency, Harvard's Children's Hospital and Harvard Divinity School, Yale School of Nursing, Princeton Theological Seminary, and to members of the NATO Intelligence Fusion Center in England. He has also spoken at the Boston Public Library's commemoration of the

Boston Marathon bombing, addressed ten thousand educators in the Air Canada Arena in Toronto, was opening keynote speaker to fifteen hundred physicians for the American Medical Directors Association, has spoken at the FBI and New York City Police Academies, led a course on resilience in Beirut for relief workers from Aleppo, Syria, and addressed caregivers in China, Vietnam, India, Thailand, Haiti, Northern Ireland, Hungary, Guatemala, Malta, New Zealand, Australia, France, England, and South Africa.

In 1994, he was responsible for the psychological debriefing of NGOs/relief workers evacuated from Rwanda during their genocide. In 1993 and again in 2001, he worked in Cambodia with professionals from the English-speaking community who were present to help the Khmer people rebuild their nation following years of terror and torture. In 2006, he also delivered presentations on self-care at the National Naval Medical Center in Bethesda, Maryland, and at Walter Reed Army Hospital to health-care professionals responsible for Iraq and Afghan war veterans. More recently, he addressed U.S. Army health-care professionals returning from Africa, where they were assisting during the Ebola crisis.

Dr. Wicks has published more than fifty books for both professionals and the general public, including the bestselling *Riding the Dragon* and *Everyday Simplicity* from Ave Maria Press. Among his latest books from Oxford University Press for the general public are *The Tao of Ordinariness, Night Call: Embracing Compassion and Hope in a Troubled World, Perspective: The Calm within the Storm*, and *Bounce: Living the Resilient Life*. His latest book on spirituality is *Heartstorming: Creating a Place God Can Call Home* (Paulist Press, 2020).

Dr. Wicks received the first annual Alumni Award for Excellence in Professional Psychology from Widener University (Chester, Pennsylvania) in 2006. He received the Humanitarian of the Year Award from the American Counseling Association's Division on Spirituality, Ethics and Religious Values in Counseling and the papal medal *Pro Ecclesia et Pontifice* from Pope St. John Paul II. In the military, Dr. Wicks was as an officer in the U.S. Marine Corps.

ALSO BY ROBERT J. WICKS
FROM PAULIST PRESS

Heartstorming provides a point of entry to the contemplative life for anyone who will become or remain open to the movements of God in their daily life. The author's forty-five field notes show what can result if the reader takes a journey of growth in being spiritually directed and then goes on to write field notes by using the simple process Wicks makes available.

Through his own experience of God's nearness and drawing from his deep understanding of the human condition, Robert Wicks puts within reach of us all a healthy spiritual perspective as part of everyday living. Dr. Wicks writes convincingly and in practical terms, giving guidance to both the spiritually adventurous and weary souls among us. In all, he emphasizes the importance of listening to the inner life—mind, will, and emotions—on our way to an increasingly fresh engagement with God's will and purposes in and around us.

RELATED BOOKS BY
ROBERT J. WICKS

Heartstorming: Creating a Place God Can Call Home

Snow Falling on Snow

Living a Gentle, Passionate Life

After 50

Prayer in the Catholic Tradition: A Handbook of Practical Approaches
  (editor)

Spiritual Resilience

Conversations with a Guardian Angel (A Novel)

No Problem: Turning the Next Corner in the Spiritual Life

Availability: The Problem and the Gift

Prayerfulness

Everyday Simplicity

Riding the Dragon

Touching the Holy

Simple Changes

*Night Call: Embracing Compassion and Hope in a
  Troubled World*

The Tao of Ordinariness: Humility and Simplicity in a Narcissistic Age

Perspective: The Calm within the Storm

Bounce: Living the Resilient Life

The Resilient Clinician

The Inner Life of the Counselor

A Primer on Posttraumatic Growth